*For my son, Jared,
and my nieces, Lindsey, Madeleine and Valen.*

Grateful Steps
1091 Hendersonville Road
Asheville, North Carolina 28803

Copyright © 2009 by Lois Chazen

Chazen, Lois
Loving Ruby

Illustrations by Sundara Fawn
Photographs by Kristi Olsen and Lois Chazen
Portraits on author and illustrator page by Rebecca D'Angelo
Portrait of Lois Chazen (Ruby on head) by Blend Photography

ISBN 978-1-935130-17-8 Hard Cover

Printed in the United States of America
Jostens, Inc.

Library of Congress Cataloging-in-Publication Data

Chazen, Lois.
  Loving Ruby / author, Lois Chazen ; illustrator, Sundara Fawn. -- 1st ed.
    p. cm.
  ISBN 978-1-935130-17-8 (hardcover : alk. paper)
  1. Cardinals (Birds)--Anecdotes. 2. Wildlife rescue--Anecdotes. I. Title.
  QL696.P2438C43 2009
  639.9'78883--dc22
                                                                        2009021926

FIRST EDITION
All rights reserved.
No part of this book may be reproduced in any manner
whatsoever without written permission from the author.

www.gratefulsteps.com

In loving memory of Dorothy Litersky, my mentor, and my beloved cat, Sagole.

Without you—Kristi, Chandler, Paula, Chuck, Kathleen and the crew at Wredes Wildlife—the rescue and release of Ruby would not have happened as it did.

My love and devotion to my family—my mother, Ellie, for her unconditional love, my father, Irv, for perseverance and perfection, my special "other" mom, Michele, for reading my manuscript over and over again, my sister, Carly, and her husband, Chris, for their enthusiasm and Barry . . . for just being my wonderful brother.

Without my Guardian Angel, Ann, my eyes would not have been opened to finding Ruby, moving to North Carolina, meeting Cindy at Kim's party, finding Micki, my publisher, and meeting Sundara. Divine timing was everything toward the publication of this heart-inspired book.

Love to all my friends, family and animals who have journeyed with me . . . and those that will.

Thank you, Dear God.

Part one . . . The beginning

Something moved in the grass as I walked in the park,
I thought it was a bird . . . perhaps a dove or lark.

It was the cutest baby bird that I've ever seen—
Too small to be on its own and probably not weaned.

In one gigantic hop with its long legs and feet,
This itsy-bitsy bird was standing in the street.

I ran to pick the bird up . . . before it was too late,
The cars stopped for me as I shouted, "Please wait."

Oh teeny-tiny baby bird . . . where's your family?
I held it in my opened hands, so it could look at me.

I brought my hands to my heart, so it could feel the beat.
The rhythm of my beating heart soon put it fast asleep.

I trusted my better judgment to take a look around.
Not one nest in a tree nor one fallen to the ground.

Just at that moment, a red cardinal swooped at me,
Perhaps that big ole' cardinal had pushed it from a tree.

I brought it to my home but knew nothing of its care.
This precious baby bird had made its nest upon my hair.

I called my friend Kristi; she would know just what to do.
She said, "Loie, I know a place you can bring the bird to."

"Just for now," Kristi said. "Bring it here so I can see.
If you want me to help, you can leave it here with me!"

As soon as I got there, Kristi noticed the crest on its head.
"It's a cardinal," she said. I replied, "The bird isn't even red!"

Oh, my! I remembered the red cardinal in the park.
It must have been the daddy, neither dove nor lark.

We didn't know if this cardinal would be a he or a she.
"Let's call it Ruby." I said, "We'll just wait and see."

I knew I needed to take Ruby back to find her family.
All I wanted was for her to be as happy as could be!

Part two . . . Help

We called Wildlife Rescue—they said bring her quick.
Ruby needed special care so she wouldn't get sick.

Wildlife Rescue told us they would show us what to do.
I knew abandoned baby birds who survived were few.

They told us what to feed her—a formula for the young.
We used a syringe to squirt the food upon her tongue.

Kristi's kitchen had become Ruby's favorite place.
Birdie mush was everywhere and even on her face.

It got pretty nasty when we had to feed her worms.
We did as we were told —it wasn't on our terms.

Now, I'm a little squeamish . . . I can't even hurt a fly.
We needed to cut the heads off, so I had to ask, "Why?"

Kristi said, "Well, if we don't cut off the worm's head,
This precious baby cardinal could possibly end up dead."

"Worms could cause problems inside a baby bird."
After that . . . I did not need to hear another word.

Ruby felt safe as she stayed around her cage.
Kristi held an oyster shell to burn a little sage.

The Indians used sage as a way to do their healing;
We were concerned about how this bird was feeling.

"I'll see you tomorrow. Bright and early I will be."
I knew I was scared to keep this baby bird with me.

I went back to see Ruby a little later than the plan.
Kristi called me to the kitchen with a knife in her hand.

"See how I cut the worm's head . . . it's like one, two, three."
"If it's so easy," I said, "please continue doing it for me."

"I'll do it for one more day, and then it's up to you."
"Okee-dokee, Kristi, but could you please make it two?"

Part three . . . My turn

We brought Ruby back to the park the very next day.
Her parents were not around; they must have flown away.

I was sad for Ruby, but now she'd be in my care.
An experience like this one would be truly rare!

I found worms in Kristi's 'fridge and snuck a little peek.
They were still from the cold, but alive—fast asleep.

Ruby said goodbye for now and gave Kristi a big kiss.
A peck from little Ruby was something not to miss.

I brought her to my home and made it cozy in her room.
I filled it up with flowered plants, so she'd enjoy the blooms.

She ate a special mushy food and worms for many days.
What a mess the room became when Ruby was at play!

Cardinals flew around outside, serenading her with songs.
She recognized these melodies and began to sing along.

Ruby would chirp away while sitting on the windowsill.
She had plenty of worms and seeds until she had her fill.

It seemed like the perfect time for Ruby to play outside.
I gently placed her in the cage and took her for a ride.

Kristi told me she was planning a big yard sale that day.
"Why don't you bring Ruby here, so we can watch her play?"

We left her cage open as we secured it in a tree.
She was now out of doors and enjoyed being "free."

We let her play all day long and then into the night.
Kristi said, "She's doing fine; I'll keep her in my sight."

I went home feeling sad and knew I would not sleep.
Ruby was now a part of me, so all I did was weep.

Part four . . . Cats

The next morning Kristi called to tell me sad news.
Ruby met her first cat and chirped the birdie blues.

Kristi opened the door to find little Ruby near his jaws
He was holding her by the tail with his furry little paws.

Ruby was taken from his mouth; wounds were slim to none.
I feared, with mangled feathers, her flying days were done.

"Come on precious little Ruby . . . I'll help you learn to fly."
With a few days of practice, she headed toward the sky.

It wasn't sky at all she saw, but a ceiling above her head.
She landed on the curtain rod above my big brass bed.

"Hooray, hooray," I shouted . . . with unbelievable bliss.
A much-desired miracle happened—I had prayed for this.

Day by day she flew some more until she got it right.
See what happens when you don't give up the fight?

I knew Ruby was happy as she played in the water.
Her bird-bath was a dish that Kristi had bought her.

She finished her bath and was soggy as a noodle.
Ruby looked funny . . . like a "cock-a-doodle-doodle".

Ruby sat on her favorite perch, as near as she could be.
I did not see my cat sneak in . . . he lunged right over me.

"Oh no, her belly's bleeding; what should I do now?"
I picked up poor Ruby and made a heart-felt vow.

"Please hang in there Ruby . . . I'll find out what to do.
I promise you little baby bird; you'll be as good as new."

Wildlife Rescue said, "Here's what you'll be needing:
Sand, baking soda or mud. Something to stop the bleeding."

I ran around my home like a chicken without a head.
I found some baking soda and did what they had said.

I held on to Ruby while I drove to the wildlife place.
All the way, tears were streaming down my face.

Part five . . . Miracles

We didn't know if the wound was from a scratch or bite.
Wildlife Rescue told me I should stay with her that night.

They also said that cat saliva was known to kill a bird.
In twenty-four hours? I couldn't believe what I heard.

Driving home I talked to her and felt such hope inside.
Ruby's will was strong enough to survive this rocky ride.

I held her in my hands, and I never left her room.
My prayers were for a miracle to whisk away her doom.

Within moments she moved and softly chirped away.
I lifted my hands in thanks for this miraculous day.

Time passed; Ruby had grown stronger in every way.
Now I would have to find a place for her to stay.

This would be the hardest time ahead I had to face.
Ruby's new home would have to be a very special place.

I knew I had options and there were more than a few;
Finding a home for Ruby would be a hard thing to do.

I called friends who own a ranch—they said she could stay.
So I began bringing Ruby there a couple times a day.

Other birds came around, but she never left my sight.
I watched every move she made, enjoying her in flight.

I finally set up her things on the big-back patio.
As much as I loved her, I would have to let her go.

Ruby's colors had changed as she got a little older;
Only her wing and tail feathers became slightly bolder.

The male cardinal's body is a deeper shade of red.
His markings are brighter, especially on his head.

Part six . . . Leaving Ruby

I would place her favorite food into her potted plant.
Ooh . . . so many worms, squiggling 'round like crazy ants.

"You must eat on your own; you're a wild bird at that.
Please stay off the ground . . . dogs also hunt like cats."

Hopping in her favorite plant, she'd wait until I'd see—
She'd pick up a squiggly worm while looking right at me.

She ate with heart's delight and then she'd fly away,
Chirping as I watched her go where she loved to play.

Her favorite perch she loved was in a mulberry tree,
Filled with sweet fruit—Ruby was happy as could be.

I was relieved to know she would finally be okay.
Ruby's call back to the wild was easier every day.

In the beginning of her release, she still came to me.
I'd feed her lots of mulberries and her favorite birdseed.

She always let me know that she loved me very much;
But Ruby no longer needed the comfort from my touch.

I thought that she was lonely as she sat upon a branch,
But there were many male cardinals visiting the ranch.

I sighed with relief and knew this would be the day.
It was just about time for Ruby to be on her way.

She flew around but not alone, and joyfully I saw
A handsome red cardinal, and all I could say was, "Ahh."

Cardinals will mate for life as they create families.
We saved precious Ruby, but now she must be free.

Somehow I knew that we'd see each other again.
Believing in miracles led me not to question "when."

I did not know the outcome but trusted with my heart.
This unbelievable ending became Ruby's beautiful start!

The End

Ruby, Ruby . . .

Where Are You?

Ruby was a fledgling when I found her. A fledgling is a fully feathered baby bird that is able to hop around and flap its wings. Initially, I had no idea what type of bird she was. The Wildlife Center confirmed that she was a cardinal based on the formation of the crest on top of her head and her distinct chirp. This is why it is important to immediately contact a Wildlife Center; they are trained to recognize the species and offer assistance in caring for birds and other animals.

Ruby was fed a type of worm called a meal-worm. When worms are fed to a fledgling, it is important to remove the head. These worms can cause many problems to the inside of the baby bird. They can destroy the stomach and also crawl back out towards the beak and suffocate the bird.

In this book, I mentioned, "smudge," a term we use when we are burning sage. There are many varieties of sage. The botanical name for "true" sage is Salvia, which means "to heal." One of the most sacred plants for the Indians is sweet-grass. As Kristi burned the sweet-grass, sage and cedar, we offered our prayers in good ways to the heavens above, while the smoke rises up to the Creator. Our tradition for healing is Native American. Ruby seemed to enjoy it. The prayers sent on Ruby's behalf were heard.

Ruby also found comfort in my hair, which probably reminded her of a cozy nest. The cardinal nest is called a cup nest and is created from bits and pieces of materials from the Earth. The cup nest is usually hidden in shrubs or trees, anywhere from three to six feet off the ground. Ruby was wandering in a small circular park around which cars were constantly moving. There was a serious risk of her being run over by a car because she could not fly. I do not encourage anyone to pick up a baby bird unless it is in danger and a nest or the parent bird cannot be located.

The cardinal is the state bird of seven states. No other bird represents so many states. The states are Illinois, Indiana, Kentucky, North Carolina, Ohio, Virginia and West Virginia. I found Ruby in a small town in Sebring, Florida, where I had been living. She still lives on the ranch where I released her and seems to be quite happy with her mate and many bird feeders. Cardinals do mate for life.

I continue to receive constant updates and photos of Ruby. When I visit her in Florida, she begins chirping as soon as I call her name. She flies around me and then perches in a nearby tree. We both stare at each other while tears of joy run down my face. She really became a miracle bird. Ruby's rescue and release took approximately three months—a little longer than usual because of the two unfortunate cat attacks.

Please put a bell on your kitty cat's collar if it will be outside. Birds need a fair warning so they may fly away before they become killed or injured.

It is a blessing to help animals—especially if you help to save their lives. I believe an animal never forgets. I know Ruby has not.

Lois Chazen currently lives in Black Mountain, North Carolina, with her Basenji, Cleo. She was born in Miami, Florida. She began writing poetry in first grade. Her passion for writing compelled her to further her education in journalism at Miami Dade Community College. She continued her studies at Florida Atlantic University in Boca Raton and received a BA in English with a strong emphasis toward creative writing.

She is currently working on a series of educational children's books called Maddy Magoo & the Alphabet Zoo. All of Lois's books help raise money for animals. Her enthusiasm for children and animals has defined the perfect life path for her. She feels the more information children receive in regard to helping our world become a better place, the more they are encouraged to make the changes needed for the animal kingdom to become stronger. Her life has been devoted to saving all species of animals. Please visit www.lovingruby.com

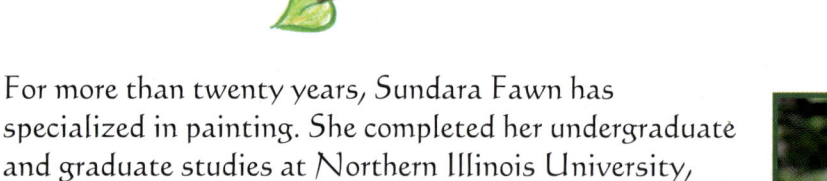

For more than twenty years, Sundara Fawn has specialized in painting. She completed her undergraduate and graduate studies at Northern Illinois University, earning BFA and MFA degrees with honors.

She creates original and commissioned works on canvas and also paints murals. Sundara has expanded her creative talents in the graphic arts field. She is skilled at book layout, mixing illustrations with art. Her current illustrations include the combination of several techniques. She incorporates photographs and original art into book illustrations, producing an extremely unique style.

Sundara lives in Asheville, North Carolina, with her daughter, Syvanah Bennett, and her dog, Nani, her best friend and hiking companion. She has a deep love for all animals and a great respect for Mother Earth. Her art can be viewed at www.sundaradesigns.com